Your Amazing Body
Ears

by Imogen Kingsley

Bullfrog Books

Ideas for Parents and Teachers

Bullfrog Books let children practice reading informational text at the earliest reading levels. Repetition, familiar words, and photo labels support early readers.

Before Reading

- Discuss the cover photo. What does it tell them?

- Look at the picture glossary together. Read and discuss the words.

Read the Book

- "Walk" through the book and look at the photos. Let the child ask questions. Point out the photo labels.

- Read the book to the child, or have him or her read independently.

After Reading

- Prompt the child to think more. Ask: What sounds do you enjoy hearing? Which sounds do you most dislike?

Bullfrog Books are published by Jump!
5357 Penn Avenue South
Minneapolis, MN 55419
www.jumplibrary.com

Library of Congress Cataloging-in-Publication Data

Names: Kingsley, Imogen, author.
Title: Ears / by Imogen Kingsley.
Description: Minneapolis, MN: Jump!, Inc. [2017]
Series: Your amazing body
"Bullfrog Books are published by Jump!"
Audience: Ages 5–8. | Audience: K to grade 3.
Includes bibliographical references and index.
Identifiers: LCCN 2016047273 (print)
LCCN 2016049074 (ebook)
ISBN 9781620316849 (hardcover: alk. paper)
ISBN 9781620317372 (pbk.)
ISBN 9781624965616 (ebook)
Subjects: LCSH: Ear—Juvenile literature.
Hearing—Juvenile literature.
Classification: LCC QP462.2 .K5645 2017 (print)
LCC QP462.2 (ebook) | DDC 612.8/5—dc23
LC record available at https://lccn.loc.gov/2016047273

Editor: Jenny Fretland VanVoorst
Book Designer: Molly Ballanger
Photo Researcher: Molly Ballanger

Photo Credits: Getty: lisagagne, 16–17. iStock: nycshooter, 6–7; Jose Girarte, 8–9; pepifoto, 12–13. Shutterstock: Celig, cover; naluwan, 1; Axel Alvarez, 3; John Panella, 4, 5; Aquila, 5; Phichai, 5; saisnaps, 5; DiversityStudio, 10; maradon 333, 10; talitha _ it, 11; motorolka, 12–13; Netta07, 12–13; Africa Studio, 14–15, 20–21; Bangkokhappiness, 14–15; espies, 14–15; Patrick Foto, 14–15; Picsfive, 14–15; RTImages, 14–15; Sedova Elena, 14–15; Tobik, 14–15; Viorel Sima, 14–15; Noam Armonn, 18; Andy Dean Photography, 19; India House, 19; alexandre zveiger, 20–21; La Gorda, 22; Napat, 23bl; Aedka Studio, 24. Thinkstock: monkeybusinessimages, 6–7.

Printed in the United States of America at Corporate Graphics in North Mankato, Minnesota.

Table of Contents

Listen Up!

Lightning strikes.

Boom!

Kit hears thunder.

It is loud.

He plugs his ears.

Honk! Honk!

Mei hears the bus.

She runs to it.

Ears help us.

How do they work?

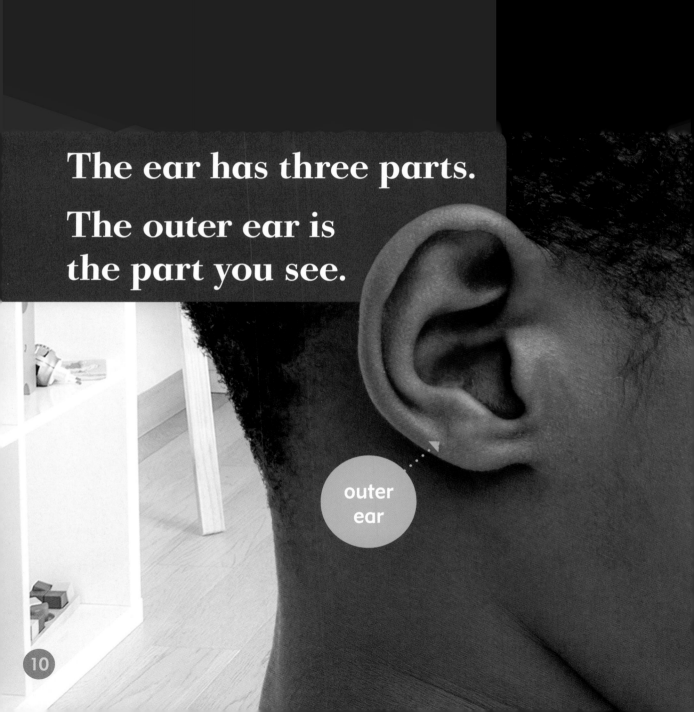

The ear has three parts.
The outer ear is
the part you see.

outer
ear

sound
waves

It works like a funnel.
It collects sound waves.

11

middle
ear

The middle ear is next.
It turns the sound
waves into vibrations.

The inner ear is last.

It sends sounds
to the brain.

This all happens
very fast.

inner
ear

When do you
use your ears?

In school.

At play.

At home.

Listen.

What do you hear?

Ears are amazing!

Parts of the Ear

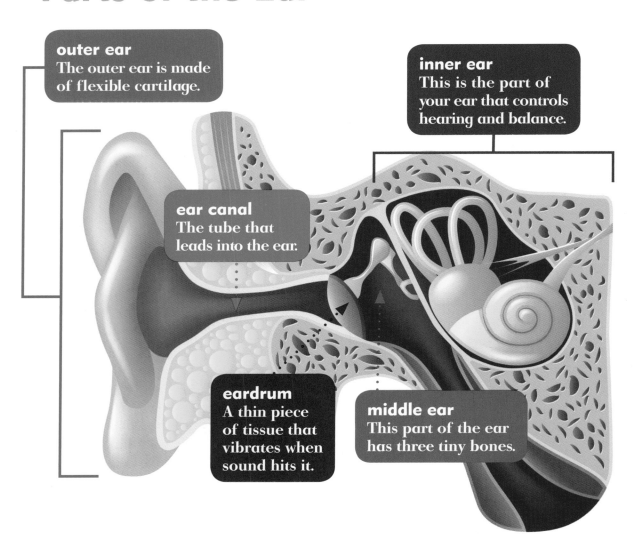

outer ear
The outer ear is made of flexible cartilage.

inner ear
This is the part of your ear that controls hearing and balance.

ear canal
The tube that leads into the ear.

eardrum
A thin piece of tissue that vibrates when sound hits it.

middle ear
This part of the ear has three tiny bones.

Picture Glossary

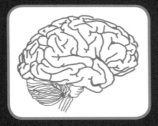

brain
The "message center" part of your body.

sound waves
An invisible wave that is made by a sound; they travel in the air.

funnel
A hollow tube that leads into something.

vibrations
Several small movements that go back and forth very fast.

Index

To Learn More

Learning more is as easy as 1, 2, 3.

1) Go to www.factsurfer.com

2) Enter "ears" into the search box.

3) Click the "Surf" button to see a list of websites.

With factsurfer.com, finding more information is just a click away.